BOARDING A MOVING TRAIN

How digital adoption makes a difference

Rephael Sweary

Co-founder and President, WalkMe

Rephael Sweary

Copyright © 2018 Rephael Sweary

All rights reserved.

ISBN:1984901087
ISBN-13: 978-1984901088

ABSTRACT

Enterprise companies are faced with an increasing pace of change and struggle to adapt to the latest technology despite its promised benefits. Yet, if truly adopted, technology is often the key to thriving among constant change. Rephael Sweary, an expert in digital adoption and user experience, discusses this problem and a possible solution.

CONTENTS

	Foreword	6
1	Boarding the Moving Train	9
2	Super-Users and Old Models	13
3	The Faulty Feedback Loop	31
4	Changing Perceptions	36
5	Rethinking User Experience	47
6	Tuning into Tech	54
7	Unlocking Potential	58

ACKNOWLEDGMENTS

Living the life of an entrepreneur while writing a book is no easy task. This book would not have been possible without the push, support, and drive of a big group of people who I highly respect, namely: Vered Shaked, Matthew Schultz, Lacie Larschan, Dannah Cahn, Jennifer Doc-Habany and Boaz Amidor for driving me to write this book. Without them, the book would have come out in 2030.

Rephael Sweary

FOREWORD

PRODUCTIVITY AND HUMAN WELL-BEING

Productivity has always been the key to improving human well-being. Prior to the agricultural revolution, people worked physically all day just to provide for their basic human survival needs. The challenges of the agricultural revolution led to the industrial revolution, whose inefficiencies are now giving rise to the digital revolution.

But something is preventing the digital revolution from fully utilizing its potential to drive productivity - the human is being ignored and left behind.

In the digital era, this means that while software is progressing very fast, employees and customers simply cannot keep pace. We are creatures of habit and we hate change. Switching from iOS to Android, for example, can be painful, and for the change to be worthwhile, we need real motivation.

I've been using Microsoft Word since 1995, the same way, every day, with no real motivation to change. The only reason I upgraded versions was if I suddenly I couldn't continue to use the software the same way unless I upgraded. At the same time, Microsoft has spent so much money and time since then on new features, but I'm blissfully unaware of any of it.

Another way to think about this is to ask yourself whether your sales people actually change their behavior with every Salesforce.com feature release. If SFDC has 3 releases per year and their R&D budget was $1.2B in 2016, are users choosing to access and use a proportionate amount of that value?

The gap between digital technology and human capabilities is growing every day and is limiting the power of productivity to increase human well-being.

At the organizational level, the digital revolution is being called digital transformation. Whether it's done in order to expand market reach, capture a competitive advantage, or as a defensive strategy, digital transformation is becoming very hard to execute.

This problem has many names within the organization - change management, adoption issues, employee onboarding, self-service adoption, etc. All these names essentially relate to the fact that it's hard for people to learn new technical skills and to change habits. I once heard from Alan Lepofsky, Vice President and Principal Analyst at Constellation Research, that people like to say that practice makes perfect - but in the digital world, practice makes habit. In all contexts with the exception of professional athletes, I could not agree with him more.

If you picked up this book, you are likely already aware at some level that digital adoption is a challenge. In this book, however, I have tried to dive more deeply into the variety of diverse factors that are driving the digital adoption challenge and to provide examples that highlight real-life aspects of the digital adoption journey.

PART I

1 BOARDING THE MOVING TRAIN

You've probably heard the joke about the Buddhist monk who goes up to a hotdog stand and says, "Make me one with everything." When he gets his hotdog, he pays with a twenty and waits for his change.

The vendor smirks and says, "Change comes from within."

Although this may be true for individuals, in business, many changes also come from without.

Technology, specifically the birth of SaaS and the shift to paperless operations, is the most significant origin of the changes we deal with in large organizations in recent decades.

Digital transformation is disrupting entire industries, starting with the pressure to implement customer-facing digital approaches, and eventually driving organizations to radically transform internal operations as well. Add to this the increasing ubiquity of SaaS systems in workplaces today, and it becomes clear that we are dealing with a new magnitude of digital challenges.

Powerful as they are, digital systems add a layer of complexity to our organizations. Gone are the days when an organization worked with one company for all its IT needs. We now pick and choose from a buffet of software solutions all provided by different vendors. Selecting the *best-of-breed* also means that we're engaged in multiple, complex adoption processes simultaneously, leading to overwhelmed and disengaged employees.

From a management perspective, becoming a digital organization means constantly trying to adapt to new technology. We are forced into a cycle where we are rarely able to achieve the stability required to fully utilize these systems. This phenomenon drives us into a vicious cycle, one in which we are constantly chasing the moving target of digital adoption. The frenzied effort involved in understanding new needs and adapting to them obscures the principle that change is constant. We find ourselves trapped in a mind-set of immediacy, focused on the one change that's happening right now rather than the big picture.

To illustrate how this plays out, imagine a mid-size business that sells school supplies. Customer concerns are straightforward and handled through email, but customer satisfaction surveys reveal that many individuals are dissatisfied with the slow reply time. In response to this problem, the business decides to plant a live chat feature on their web page.

The company shops around for a vendor, makes a selection, and begins to roll out the new system. The platform is relatively simple, after a few weeks employees get the hang of it. The problem is solved...for the moment.

At the same time, the company releases a new product: a smart binder. This binder-tablet hybrid is expensive and feature-rich. Suddenly, the chat feature isn't sufficient means to support customer inquiries. They want a phone call.

The smart binder creates a new issue for the company. While they once got by using only the chat platform, they now need a CRM system to log the large numbers of calls they are receiving daily. Another selection and adoption process begins. Software training starts over from square one.

This is the reality with which businesses are living. There is never quite enough time to adapt to the current paradigm before a sudden change disrupts it. We are chasing our own tails.

I've often compared digital adoption to boarding a moving train. It sounds daunting because it is. The "tech train" is moving whether we like it or not. To board a moving train, you must first pick up speed by running at a clip alongside the car as you prepare yourself to leap. Then, you brace yourself for the jolt of the landing.

Most of us are still walking, and we're certainly not prepared for the jolt.

Digital adoption, as a subject of inquiry and concern, remains marginalized in large organizations. It is easier to just grin and bear it, so to speak, than to address the issue. In my experience, however, I have discovered that many executives, when asked about digital adoption, have a great deal to say.

Upper management aren't the only ones feeling the drag. Across industries, and irrespective of position, employees and leadership at large organizations have stories to tell of the woes of digital adoption. I have heard tales about employees' inability to master a new technology, about their difficulty finding support. I've seen cases in which employees who don't recognize the power of a new software develop hostile feelings to the new technology and nostalgia for the old system.

Leadership, in many cases, is unaware of the challenges of digital adoption. I have also seen on occasion leadership who is aware of the phenomenon—but who don't know the first step of how to approach it.

These professionals admit that it takes almost a year for a new employee to master the required systems, and that this process causes considerable overwhelm for staff members. A year is a long time, especially in an economy that has seen more and more individuals hopping from job to job, often spending only a year or two at any given organization.

Something in the digital adoption process is less straightforward than we feel it "should be." Meanwhile, technology increasingly infiltrates daily operations, and the digital adoption problem grows in significance.

As organizations continue to invest in new digital systems, the fact that technology is not fully adopted poses a threat to business success. Enterprises stand to sink hundreds of thousands, if not millions of dollars into the most sophisticated digital systems—whether or not they are used to their potential. Additionally, the opportunity cost of training time spent on these systems racks up an equally significant price tag.

The fruits of the digital revolution are in our hands and yet, somehow, we are not tasting them.

So what's holding us back?

The purpose of this book is to explore this question and to offer solutions. Digital adoption is rarely a primary area of concern for organizations. But as we struggle to make the most of our digital investments, the time has come for an understanding of the adoption process—an in depth look at the unique challenges this process entails. Once leadership brings awareness and foresight to the adoption journey, we can start to do meaningful work to transform our relationship with technology.

2 SUPER-USERS AND OLD MODELS

The MacGyver Approach

Apple loves sleek, simplified product design. We see it in their laptops, smartphones, and their tablets. Apple has become a giant in the market for the quality of these products as well as their ability to function as fashion statements.

But what happens when a design is too sleek?

I'll tell you: it gets lost in the couch cushions.

I'm speaking about the remote control for the Apple TV. Roughly the size of a teaspoon, this remote is silver, elegant, and slender. With only two buttons and four arrows, it is a far cry from the traditional TV remote—heavy, black, and burdened with countless buttons that most of us will only ever use by mistake—like in *Friends* when Ross's pet monkey accidentally changes the TV to Spanish dubbing and no one can figure out how to turn it back.

The Apple remote has no mysterious buttons and functions according to a simple, intuitive logic. But there is a flipside to this kind of design.

This minimalist and easy-to-use device is probably the most easily lost remote in the history of home entertainment. It slips between couch cushions with the greatest ease, or else silently drops from the coffee table where it is thin enough to get wedged between the rug and the floor.

A friend of mine in New York explained this to me as she showed me her latest invention. She called it the "Flashremote." Created by attaching the tiny remote to a massive flashlight with duct tape, the Flashremote ensured that she would never again have to plumb the couch cushions in desperation. It was a crude device, and certainly beneath the design standards of Apple—but it did the job flawlessly.

My friend even went on to tell me that the Flashremote had solved two problems. Power-outages aren't rare in New York, and it proves handy to have the flashlight end of the Flashremote nearby—instead of having to dig through the closet for it with no light.

It's always gratifying to see innovation at work in everyday life, and this was the perfect "MacGyvering" of an everyday problem.

What does it mean to MacGyver something? The name-turned-verb comes from the 1985 hit TV series MacGyver, which followed the adventures of secret agent Angus MacGyver. The show is largely remembered for the unique approach MacGyver took towards getting himself out of tight spots, which usually involved brilliantly repurposing an everyday object in an innovative way.

Decades after MacGyver retired from shorting missile timers with paperclips, fashioning pieces of bubble gum into explosives, and deflecting laser beams with broken binoculars—"to MacGyver" something has come to mean using an everyday item in an expansive and innovative manner.

You can MacGyver a broken chair by rigging it together with a shoelace, or turn a coat hanger into a device to get your dropped keys out from under a parked car. MacGyvering is an approach rather than an action—a mindset that sees the potential in ordinary objects—reconfiguring and combining them to great effect. But for every MacGyver out there, there are about a thousand more anti-MacGyvers doing just the opposite.

Somewhere there is a man who uses his smartphone as a regular phone, except occasionally using the built-in calculator to figure out the tip at a restaurant. There is a woman who purchased an expensive and highly versatile laptop, but uses it only to check her email. Here are two individuals who are losing economic value by underutilizing complex and expensive technology, and missing out on functionality.

But while consumers like these lose out on both finance and function, it's nothing compared to the losses incurred by large organizations if they fail to make the most of their tech.

Large organizations are making increasingly significant investments in tech, with good reason. Making the most of available technology is essential to surviving and growing in today's market. But these investments are not without risk. When organizations invest big, they are banking on large increases in performance and business success.

So how can they guarantee that they will see the return on investment?

It is all a matter of approach. Someone with a MacGyver sensibility would be able to take a paperclip and turn it into a CRM. But what happens when the staff of a large organization takes a CRM and turns it into a paperclip?

Turning a CRM into a Paperclip

Information technology is all around us and constantly developing to be faster and more comprehensive. Tech has become an essential part of our lives and businesses. For individuals, digital tools are largely a matter of convenience and entertainment. For large organizations, however, tech is absolutely vital. In this day and age every company is becoming a technology company. Whether or not a business makes use of available tech is the difference between staying competitive and falling behind, between growth and stagnation, between thriving and surviving.

Despite this, organizations large and small are failing to make use of technological innovation, although not for lack of trying. We are purchasing tech and using tech, but we're not really getting as much out of it as one would assume. The phenomenon has been dubbed "the Productivity Paradox."

The theory known as the Productivity Paradox was first articulated in 1987 when Robert Solow, a prominent American economist, made a startling observation. As information technologies began to rapidly develop and change the landscape of how American industries operated, one would expect to see a corresponding series of leaps in job growth, the GDP, and salaries. But Solow saw no such leaps and remarked famously that "you can see the computer age everywhere but in the productivity statistics."

It was true. The 70's and 80s's saw productivity stagnation, contrary to most economists' projections. Across the country economists began theorizing about the so-called Productivity Paradox. It was perplexing—why hadn't the radical advent of IT caused a boost in the U.S. economy? Such boosts had typically accompanied developments in technology throughout the nineteenth century; the lightbulb permitted work at all hours, the steam engine accelerated trade, and the telephone gave us instantaneous long-distance communication.

The paradox has only become more puzzling with time. Solow's observation that the computer age could be seen "everywhere" in 1987 sounds almost quaint. It would have been impossible back then to imagine just how ubiquitous IT would be in 2017. For thirty years economists have kicked this theory around and generated various explanations—many of these going so far as to say that perhaps the Internet just isn't as revolutionary as we assumed it would be.

This, to me, sounds like an exaggeration. We know that the Internet is revolutionary and we feel its power and influence in our lives every day. But there's a contradiction between our experience and the numbers, as if we've stumbled into some kind of economic Bermuda Triangle. We are missing an input into the equation.

Most likely there isn't one single solution to the problem, but a constellation of contributing factors. One amongst them being that there seems to be a gap between the revolutionary potential of tech and what we actually do with it. As the wise teacher, Mr. Feeny, said in the classic coming-of-age sitcom, Boy Meets World, "Guttenberg's generation thirsted for a new book every six months. Your generation gets a new webpage every six seconds. And how do you use this technology? To beat King Koopa and save the princess." In short, we have access to technology's potential—but we're not doing enough with it.

We know what the MacGyvers in our organizations are up to. If they can turn a paperclip into a CRM, just imagine what they can do with an actual CRM! There may also be a few Mr. Feenys roaming the halls and trying to get everyone to wake up and smell the technological potential. But what about everyone else?

The Old Model

Denise calls herself an "old model." When I ask her to explain she says, "They don't make 'em like me anymore. I prefer to write with a pen and paper instead of typing, and prefer to call rather than email. I sometimes think that I was born in the wrong generation."

Denise's attitude towards technology is nothing new, but it is surprising considering how young she is. At 28, Denise is considered a digital native. She was raised with computers and has had a smartphone for a decade now. Still, she finds herself put off by digital media and computers.

She recently started a new job at UCLA doing fundraising for the university. She was hired because of her background in non-profit administration. She wasn't hired for being a tech expert. In fact, over the course of three job interviews, the subject of technology never came up.

Now she's feeling overwhelmed. "The job is tech!" she says. "Everything we do has its own platform. There's like six different systems I'm trying to learn. I thought I was alone in the struggle, but when I turned to co-workers for help, they were mostly as clueless as me."

After looking for help from her peers, she finally consulted with her manager and admitted that she was struggling to master the large range of new systems and technologies that she is expected to use.

"Don't worry about it," her boss said. "It takes people about six to eight months to get the hang of it."

Denise was surprised by the answer. It seemed like an awfully long time to get people on board with technologies that are, after all, supposed to make us work *more efficiently*.

Super-Users

I continued my inquiry by speaking with Stephen Schultz, Director of Business Development at Supporting Strategies, a provider of outsourced bookkeeping services. His role involves both selling franchises and helping new franchisees as they set up their practice, hire staff, and begin selling their services.

When I asked him what it takes to successfully adopt tech, he told me that what he needs are "Super-Users." Schultz explained that most "Technology has gotten to a point where it's so very intuitive and easy to use that no one actually needs to read an instruction manual for anything anymore. You just take your new computer out of the box and start working with it. No training or anything. That's great."

According to Schultz, this can also pose a problem. This kind of intuitive interface makes it very easy for anyone to become a competent user, but we don't want just competent users. They're not the ones transforming the potential value of technology into reality.

Schultz himself is a self-declared Super-User. With a background in engineering and a genuine excitement for discovering a great new software or application, he loves to tinker with technology. "I want to know what every icon in the toolbar means and what it does. I want to know every feature available so that when I run into a problem, I know how to troubleshoot for myself."

What does it take to be a Super-User? It comes down to curiosity and trust. "You've got to trust the software developers. If you're having a problem with something in Hubspot CRM, one of my favorite tools, you're probably not the first person who has had that problem and the developers have probably created a solution for you already. That's the trust. The curiosity, then, is the ability to start clicking different buttons to find it."

However, employees at Supporting Strategies aren't hired because they're Super-Users— nor should they be. They're hired to be great bookkeepers and salespeople.

"With Hubspot CRM, I can write and save templated emails and sequences of emails. If it's something I'm sending out more than once, I have a template for it. That way I can create the perfect email for a situation and never have to rewrite it from scratch. It's a tool that automates a lot of what we do as salespeople—but the end goal of automation isn't just automation."

As a true New Englander, Schultz ends all his emails with "Go Pats!" as a sign off. "My emails are me, natural and personal."

"When my franchisees ask me to write their templated emails for them, I get the idea that they're missing the point. They're not making the most of the tool. They don't want to engage with it. When they ask me for a document that I know is saved in Hubspot, I get frustrated. They could go find that document themselves, but they still resist interacting with the software. They want to do things their own way, like asking me to send a document by emailing it to them as an attachment, a process that feels more comfortable. Or they expect that the software will come in and act for them without them having to be in the driver's seat."

What this shows is that they aren't Super-Users. They don't see the power of a CRM. Moreover, they don't understand a CRM at all.

We have an issue here. To use a cliché, you can lead a horse to water but you can't make him drink. A great CRM can really enhance how a sales team does business. But what tool do you use to get your sales team to engage with the CRM in the first place?

The Reality in Which We Live

The story of Denise anticipating a 6-8-month learning period for the many new software programs and databases required by her new position at UCLA highlights the reality of how employees are relating to and learning enterprise software systems.

According to statistics compiled by Deloitte, more than 80% of companies rate the work they do as "complex" or "highly complex" for their employees. Today, the average US employee works 47 hours per week, while 49% of them work 50 or more and 20% of workers are working 60 hours or more. What's more, productivity statistics have shown that productivity in the US has slowed to a crawl since 2011.

A great deal of this complexity, difficulty, and stagnation is stemming from technology that is supposed to simplify our organizations. This is a clear illustration of the Productivity Paradox—the gap between tech's potential and what we actually do with it. These are startling conclusions. We have at our disposal a range of fantastic tools that are supposed to help us work faster, easier, and smarter. But we are spending more time in the office than ever, and we're not even seeing a comparable increase in productivity.

Let's return to Denise, who was hired for her intelligence, experience, and capabilities. She has been outfitted with a number of technologies designed to put her skills into action. But these tools are slowing her down, and making her feel overwhelmed. Denise herself would say that we should scrap it all. Bring back the pen, paper and the filing cabinet.

But scrapping our current digital systems is hardly necessary. We can, actually, have our technological cake and eat it too. To do so we must understand what our employees are going through when we ask them to get up to speed with a new technology.

The Forgetting Curve

I don't need to tell anyone that training is valuable. We know this, and it's why we are so ready to invest money and time into this effort. And we definitely are investing. According to Training Magazine's annual research, the average training budget for companies with 10,000+ employees was $14.3 million in 2016. This is to say nothing of the time investment, which also comes down to dollars and cents in the end.

The issue really begins with how we think about training. Perhaps we've internalized the scene from *The Matrix* where Neo downloads Kung Fu abilities to his brain—mastering in just a few seconds a craft that would normally take a lifetime to learn.

Is this what we think is happening when we train employees? If so, we're a long way off. And yet we see over and over again that training programs are designed as a single event, or at the very maximum a cluster of events. A series of videos or modules are watched, information is dispersed, and maybe a few webinars are thrown in for good measure. Time, money and resources are spent on pushing employees through a training conveyer belt, after which the employees are presumed to be done learning the system.

But as it turns out, the average employee only retains about 20% of the knowledge learned during a training session. Six months in and they'll be in need of a review for some of the most basic features of the new system.

This is because, as humans, our learning curve is also a forgetting curve. New knowledge takes time to gain a real foothold because we're constantly forgetting certain elements and having to reacquire them. The concept of the forgetting curve attempts to create a formula for this process. But the rate of forgetting will always be affected by different factors.

One of these factors is personal. Each person will have their own learning style. Based on their natural predilection for tech, each employee will have a different experience learning new technology. Not only does this vary from person to person, but it also varies from industry to industry. A high-tech company, for instance, may draw in a technologically fluent staff—but even here we will see a diverse range of aptitudes amongst employees.

Another factor which affects the retention of learned material is the perceived meaningfulness of the information. If I gave you three words to remember, words that had no personal significance to you (let's say "condor, stamp, elegance"), chances are you would not be able to remember all three a month later. Maybe you would have forgotten them by the end of the day. But what if I have told you three words of deep, personal significance? Say they were names of your aunts or your three best friends. You would probably be able to remember. But meaningfulness isn't just about personal connection. It's also about perceived value. If I gave you the first words again, the ones you have no connection to, but told you that if you remember them in a month you'll get a check for a million dollars – I don't think you'd have much trouble.

This issue of engagement is huge. How often are we forgetting to impart to our employees the hugely important, big-picture value of a new technology?

Significance is a Two-Way Street

Much of what bookkeepers do is data-entry, but automation has removed a lot of that from the bookkeeping process in recent years, allowing bookkeepers to take on a new role for their clients. The way Jorgenson and Schultz see it, the bookkeepers at Supporting Strategies are numbers analysts rather than number-crunchers. They are business consultants—counsellors who advise their clients on the financial wellbeing of their businesses.

Leslie Jorgenson and Steve Schultz saw a presentation for HubDoc at a tradeshow and had immediately recognized what a powerful and helpful tool this could be for their company. Essentially it would help empower employees to move down a path with less number pushing and more time attributed to consulting. It wasn't until they tried to roll out HubDoc at Supporting Strategies that they encountered first-hand the issue of significance.

"HubDoc does a lot of things," Jorgenson said. Ultimately it is like a smart-filing cabinet. It makes it easy to upload all important documents into one platform and then synthesize and extract that data when you need it."

Jorgenson and Schultz were sold on HubDoc. Who wouldn't love this? It then came time to introduce the new tool to their employees.

Jorgenson put together what she described as a "whole dog and pony show" to unroll the new software. She expected to see the kind of enthusiasm from her staff that she herself felt about HubDoc. But this was not the reaction she got. She described the staff's response as "crickets." In other words, they did not share her excitement.

At first, using HubDoc was not mandatory for the staff. No one had expected that it would need to be. Jorgenson and Schultz had expected that everyone would want in right away. But as time went by, they began to realize just how few people on staff were using this tool.

As it turned out, the staff's attitude toward the platform was fearful and hostile. The bookkeepers, paid hourly, saw automation as a threat to their pay checks. While they agreed that this would allow them to do their job faster, they didn't agree that this was a good thing. The bottom line was, they didn't see the *personal significance* of the new technology.

After a few months, the company changed its approach to HubDoc. They made a greater attempt to present the new tech in a way that would highlight its significance to the employees. Yes, they said, this will mean that you spend less hours on each client. But it also means that you will have more time available to take on new clients, and that the time you do spend on each client will not be tied up in frustrating data-entry tasks. They were starting to make progress.

But then something else happened. Jorgenson, on holiday vacation in Denmark with her family, received a call. It was one of her employees who was confused about how to use a certain HubDoc feature.

It's true, motivation and significance are the first barriers we have to pass when getting a staff on board with a new technology. But on the other side of these barriers is the adoption process itself.

This brings us to the next issue that our employees are dealing with: support.

Desperately Seeking Support

Calling the CEO for a small support issue with your workplace software is a bit like calling the Post Master General to ask when your Amazon purchase will arrive. It highlights an issue that many employees at all kinds of organizations are dealing with: they don't know where to turn for assistance.

If we're still thinking about training like downloading Kung Fu, there's no need for support. The employees have been taught everything they need, and now they can move on and put the information to good use. But this just isn't the case. Our employees are individuals. Sometimes the knowledge won't click, and sometimes it will click but not stick.

So what do our employees do when they have trouble? A Super-User may be able to troubleshoot his or her own issues. But what about the rest of us? Denise mentioned that first she went to co-workers who had been there longer than she had, but most of them were just as confused as she was. Then she went to her boss, who told her to just stick it out.

This may have reassured her that the trouble she was having was normal and would pass, but it certainly didn't bring her any answers. And in the meantime, she's sitting in an office eight hours a day and is expected to be doing work. Still new at the organization, she wants to impress, not flounder. And in order to do that, she needs to know how to use all the tech that she's expected to be using.

Denise, despite being tech-resistant, is exactly the kind of employee that large organizations want and need. She's capable, energetic, and hardworking. What's more, she really cares about the university she works for. When her boss told her to be patient and wait six to eight months, she didn't just get worried for herself, she got worried for the whole organization.

"There's high turnover," she told me. "People come and work for a year and then move on to something else. That means that for some employees, the university is investing in eight months of what is essentially a training period for an employee who will only be working a few months after that period ends."

The issue of high-turnover is common to many organizations: millennials, making up the largest percentage of the workforce, commonly change jobs every two to three years. According to a survey by Future Workplace, ninety-one percent of millennials (born between 1977 and 1997) expect to stay in a job for less than three years. However, even if this weren't an issue, all employers would be better off if their employees were working at peak efficiency from day one.

As leaders we are asking employees to trust us when we roll out a new technology. We want them to trust that the new tech is for their own good as well as for the good of the company. But something is getting lost along the way. Our training programs are producing employees who don't know where to turn for support, don't believe in the "help" button, and more seriously, who don't know why they're using the technology in the first place.

These factors are all barriers to successful adoption.

But all the motivation and support in the world will still be ineffective if the software itself is inherently challenging for employees. As Steve Schultz said, we are a society raised on intuitive tech. The days of saving the user manual are behind us. So what exactly happens when employees show up and find software far more sophisticated than the tech they've encountered as consumers?

The UX Paradox

Consumers are being sold a dream about Information Technology. The dream is that tech is seamless, easy to use, and intuitive. We are sold this dream by our phone companies, our retailers, our content providers, and our banks. But this dream, while it may be true enough on the consumer end, is far from the reality of tech experienced by employees of large organizations.

For the learning division at a company like T-Mobile, this disconnect between user-friendly consumer tech and enterprise software is a major area of concern. While the consumers themselves, who are the main goal and beneficiary of T-Mobile's increasingly digital operations, may not feel this effort—it is definitely felt on the employee's end.

As VP of Learning Development at T-Mobile, Scott Tweedy was the first to introduce new employees to the digital component of their work.

"When they show up they're so excited," Scott says. "But then they get here and we put them in training and they're looking at a screen that's a little north of a green screen. It's not pretty… they think: this is T-Mobile?"

According to Tweedy, it takes eight weeks to get a front-line representative ready to have their first interaction with a customer. But most of that time is spent teaching them to navigate systems. "We're not really talking about the product, which is what's most important. It's about how you get through this craziness to get to the product."

Compared to the super intuitive technology we use in our personal lives, enterprise systems continue to lag behind in user-friendliness.

We're left with a problem of expectations. Our staff is used to consumer tech and thus expects user-friendliness. But as we saw with Denise, this is not what they get.

In the Zen tradition, there is a concept of "beginner's mind." When we begin a new practice, whether it's learning a new language, instrument, or working at a new job, this is the time when our mind is most awake. Without expectations and habits, we stay present with what we are doing rather than snapping into autopilot.

Being a beginner is challenging. This aspect of difficulty is, in itself, a form of training. When a student begins learning how to play guitar, for example, his or her mind is attentive. A new chord, when it's first played, will feel like a bizarre and unnatural contortion of the hand. But with time, repetition, and focus, this chord will begin to become second nature.

When the player then begins to learn an even more difficult chord, he or she won't be expecting ease, but instead, will be familiar with the discomfort of challenge. This is significant. It means that when the player first tries to spread their fingers with dexterity across five frets, he or she might feel frustration but also knows that, eventually, there will be a payoff.

It will get easier.

Now imagine this process through the lens of consumer technology.

Imagine if anyone who picked up a guitar found that they could play a number of basic songs with no training whatsoever. This user-friendly, intuitive guitar would allow anyone to master the standard campfire classics with ease.

But then, when the user tries to play something outside of this repertoire, they will encounter difficulty for the first time. Their hands will hurt. The sound will come out uneven and off-tune. As beginners they had no trouble whatsoever and now, suddenly, they have lost their rock star status.

Most of us, in this situation, would return to the safety of the intuitive, beginner's repertoire. Without any sense that this difficulty will lead anywhere (to mastery), why suffer? After all, we already have enough songs to have a nice little singalong and impress our friends.

This is exactly the position employees currently find themselves in with a great deal of enterprise software.

There is no focus required of us when using consumer technology. There is no sense of overcoming of obstacles, and very little troubleshooting. This means that when we encounter challenging software at work, we quickly become frustrated.

This frustration happens when an individual switches from simple consumer tech at home to complex enterprise tech when they clock in. Many software systems used by employees are simple up to a point, but become challenging when the user attempts to do anything more advanced than the most basic functions.

Struggling to get past the proficiency plateau has been my own experience with Microsoft Word. I've used Microsoft Word for decades. I've used it so much, in fact, that if it had been a guitar instead of a word processor, I would probably be on a world tour right now. And yet, I'm no master. Microsoft Word, as a basic typing software, has a training time of 1 second. If you know how to type, you know how to use Word. It wasn't until I was trying to format a long and complex document last year that I realized how little I understood about this software.

Difficulties with formatting and creating a table of contents caused me huge frustration. I had been using Word for two decades without ever trying to do something complex. Why couldn't they have worked all this out before it became a problem for me?

I turned to Google for support, and came across a few forums discussing the exact issue I was dealing with. Turns out that the people at Microsoft had worked out these issues. It was then that I first started glancing at the Microsoft Word's toolbar cluttered with dozens of little icons and buttons. It dawned on me that each one of those buttons did something. I began to play around with all of them.

In the twenty years since I started using Microsoft Word, teams of experts and geniuses at Microsoft had been engaged in a nonstop effort to improve the software's functionality. Countless updates and new versions, and better features had been released —all intended to benefit me, the user. But I had been using Word the same way I used it on day one. I had fallen into the trap of plateauing at competency.

It's not as though we haven't seen progress in the area of enterprise tech UX. User experience designers have done a pretty good job at simplifying the user experience. The computers of the 80's were massive in scale, not to mention the equally cumbersome software. It was only the solitary IBM technician, armed with specialized training and preparation, who had the power to tame the beast.

For every software we use you can be sure that there is a highly skilled team of individuals somewhere working tirelessly to deliver us a better user experience. They want their product to be slick, easy to use, and intuitive so that users can make the most of its benefits and get on with their core work.

They've made great progress. Today's software is carefully designed with the human user in mind, but we still have a problem.

Perhaps you are familiar with Zeno's Paradox. According to this logical paradox, if one were to stand ten feet from a wall and decide to walk to that wall, he or she would first have to arrive halfway before getting all the way there. So one walks five feet, and now five feet remain between the person and the wall. Now to cover this last five feet one will still have to go halfway before getting all the way there. This is simple logic. So one walks 2.5 feet. This process of division by halves will continue until the individual is so close to the wall as to touch it—though logically he or she can never actually arrive.

I propose a similar theory, which I'll call the UX Paradox. While UX will continue to develop in comprehensiveness and ease-of-use for each one of the software systems at use in a given organization, we have yet to see it arrive to, or even get close to, the point at which adoption becomes an intuitive and smooth process.

This is for two main reasons: the first being that absolute standards of UX don't exist.

No matter how intuitive a system's UX may be, it will always only be intuitive according to that system's own internal logic. The diversity of systems at use in any given organization thus present a barrier to skilled technical use. Each system will have its own platform design, method of login, password requirements, and general style of use.

The second reason is the dynamic internal development of the software itself. The platform will continue to evolve. New features will come out and other features will disappear or be modified. The nature of UX is to evolve, and this evolution of UX within a platform can become a barrier to skilled technical use of the platform.

Were these systems static, we could expect employees to eventually "master" them. This is not the case. Not only are these systems dynamic, but organizations are dynamic. Thus the body of knowledge and knowhow needed to use these systems is also dynamic—a fact which, for the overwhelmed employee, can be quite distressing.

The sum total of these problems – overwhelm and motivation, training and support, and expectations and ease-of-use—is a significant obstacle for any large organization attempting to successfully adopt new technology. But so far we have spoken only about the obstacles experienced by employees. We must also consider the lack of organizational awareness and transparency for the new technology usage – an issue of equal importance that can undermine leadership's adoption efforts if left unaddressed.

3 THE FAULTY FEEDBACK LOOP

A Problem at City Hall

There's a controversy going on at the City Hall in Boston—a controversy which has raged for decades with no signs of slowing down. But unlike many governmental controversies, this one has nothing to do with what goes on *inside* city hall. It's not about corruption or unpopular policy decisions. Nope, in Boston the controversy at City Hall is the City Hall building itself.

Built in 1968, it is a prominent and illustrative example of Brutalism—an architectural movement which favored heavy, concrete structures on a massive scale. The distinctive design is still widely hailed by architects, historians and academics. Unfortunately, the public itself has never much loved this public building. In fact, they hate it.

Trends come and go, and architecture is subject to the same winds of change as fashion, but concrete is sturdier than denim. The remnants of the Brutalist movement are still with us, even if the trend has long died out. This, according to architect Mark Kushner, is one of the central problems of architecture: it has a faulty feedback loop.

Kushner, an architect, author, speaker and pioneer of architecture's digital transformation, has articulated this issue in both his TED talk and book, "The Future of Architecture in 100 Buildings." His theory goes something like this: an architect designs a building and construction then begins. This construction process is slow. It may take years. It certainly takes a lot of effort, money and material. During the time in which the building is being constructed, the same architect may design ten more buildings and break ground on those projects as well. Finally, when construction is completed on the first building, the public has a chance to react.

In the case of the Boston City Hall, the reaction was largely negative. This feedback gets back to the architects, but what do they then do with it? The building is already complete. A feedback loop is in place, but it's not really operating if it doesn't give architects and planners the chance to make use of the new information and readjust their course.

Not all feedback is created equal. There are some aspects of a business for which we have developed incredibly fast and functional feedback loops. One such area is marketing. If an organization goes forward with a radical new marketing campaign, there will be a significant investment of time, resources, and money. What happens if the campaign is a flop? It's not possible to recover the investment entirely, but an organization's success will depend on its ability to monitor its new investments, make accurate projections, gather data and readjust its course accordingly. In other words, if the new marketing campaign is a flop it's far better to find out sooner rather than later.

As much of marketing has moved into the online realm, myriad tools have entered the scene providing crucial analytics about the impact of our marketing efforts. We're able to see how many clicks and page visits we get. Not only this, we can see where these clicks and page visits are coming from. We can gather data about the specific individuals who are responding to our marketing efforts and refine our approach accordingly. And this is only the tip of the iceberg. Today, immediately after an organization launches a marketing campaign, it begins receiving feedback.

But while the advent of analytics has been pivotal in the evolution of marketing and sales, almost all of these advances have been geared towards analyzing customer behavior. If these outward, market-focused feedback loops are critical for success, where is the feedback loop that telling us how our staff is responding to new tech?

Speaking more with Leslie Jorgenson, she told me how she started

Supporting Strategies in 2004 and how they have expanded greatly since. With more offices popping up in more states, and an expanded range of services, they looked to technology to help in managing operations for each new level of growth.

The decision to embrace new technology has been a boon for the organization. Jorgenson has seen firsthand how Hubspot CRM has changed the way her company does sales for the better. In addition to this, she made a decision to develop a custom internal use software for the business, called Workplace, as a way of getting their many offices, spread out across states and territories, onto the same page.

"This was huge for us," Jorgenson said of the decision to develop Workplace. It was their own custom software and cost hundreds of thousands to create. It's a shared space where anyone from our team can go in and see everything that's going on operationally. It handles task management, time tracking, documentation—things like that." But after rolling it out to all the franchise owners, it was hard to keep tabs on the relationship the staff had with the system.

It wasn't until a small crisis at one of the franchise offices that Jorgenson got some insight into this blind spot. "One of our franchisees had a manager who had been very overwhelmed for a number of weeks. She wasn't performing well, she was very stressed out, and then one day she just quit. We wanted to ensure that despite the sudden change that everything would continue smoothly for the clients at this office."

The first thing Jorgenson did was to check in on the office's Workplace account. What she found was that the software was underused and in disarray. "Nothing was there, nothing was logged, and nothing was organized."

What had occurred was a cycle in which the manager was overwhelmed because the office wasn't staying organized with Workplace, and the office wasn't staying organized with Workplace because the manager was overwhelmed. What Jorgenson had just encountered was that her tech had a faulty feedback loop and lacked a means of getting information back to the source.

The crisis ended up being a great source of insight. Because of the sudden departure of a manager—a problem had been brought to light.

In other words, the crisis itself had created a feedback loop.

But what if this crisis hadn't happened? And what about the many franchise locations who hadn't faced such a crisis? The absence of a crisis is not indicative of a healthy relationship of the staff and the Workplace software. The software may still be underused or misunderstood. In this sense, the feedback loop isn't functioning. And when the feedback loop fails to function, there is no way for an organization to alter its course or to save its investment in software.

PART II

4 CHANGING PERCEPTIONS

Living within Technology

We're in uncharted terrain. Our IT spend is high and growing, but our investment is threatened by the pitfalls of the digital adoption process. What's more, the lack of a feedback loop prevents us from raising awareness and responding to these issues.

Despite this, our approach towards digital adoption has yet to become a serious subject of inquiry for many large organizations. This is a mistake. We need to bring attention to the expanding nature of our relationship with technology. Our attitudes towards technology are outdated, and they must evolve.

To understand what I mean by this, let's take a look back at how things used to be when technology was merely *with* us, but not *all around us*. It was a time of landline phones, simple cellphones, desktop computers, CD players, word processing software, and America Online. This was the era before smartphones and Wi-Fi. We used the Internet for many things, but not for everything.

It was a time when technology *did things*. Today's tech does not "do things." It does *anything*—or is at least moving in that direction. Once upon a time, technology served merely a supplemental role in our lives, speeding up or enhancing what we were already doing but not creating new paradigms.

Much of the technology in this period had some corollary in another, older technology. It was an upgrade rather than a radical new development. The CD player came in and displaced the cassette tape which had displaced the clunky, non-portable record player. The DVD came and did the same thing to the VHS. Our computers, for quite some time, were used in most houses as a replacement for typewriters and mailboxes.

This is no longer the situation. Today we do not live *with* technology. We live *within* technology. Tech, instead of being a set of tools and gadgets at our disposal, is a framework *within* which we accomplish a great deal of everything that we do. We educate ourselves and others online. We learn online. We research online. We shop online, we sell online, we communicate online, we conduct our banking, bookkeeping and our accounting online, and we even date and socialize online. The list goes on.

The ubiquity of the internet has brought about a relationship between us and technology that is totally immersive. The dynamic is comparable to how a city's inhabitant might interact with the city's infrastructure. For example, a New Yorker grabbing a coffee at his local bodega won't spare a thought for the unspeakably massive network of infrastructure (which enables telecommunications, the delivery of utilities, and transportation) lying right beneath their feet and around them all on sides.

This infrastructure supports and contains the actions of a New Yorker's daily life. It is so very immersive and present that the savvy city dweller won't even notice it, like the proverbial fish who doesn't know what water is.

But we continue to conceptualize technology as something we live *with*—and it seems to me that this misconception is one of our barriers to adoption.

The Cardboard Box Principle

Imagine that you're a pilot. Your plane has just crash-landed in the Sahara Desert. Thousands of miles away from any human settlement on

Earth, you are utterly stranded and alone. And then, suddenly, you hear a voice:

"Draw me a sheep."

This is the puzzling situation in which the narrator of the children's classic, "The Little Prince," finds himself. A mysterious child approaches him from across the sands and, rather than asking for water or exclaiming, "I'm lost!" requests a drawing of a sheep.

The narrator, sufficiently baffled, decides to play along. He draws a sheep in his notepad and hands it to the boy.

"No, no," the boy says. "This sheep is too old."

The man draws a second sheep.

"No, no," the boy says. "This one is sick."

The man draws a third sheep.

"No, no," the boy says. "This is a ram. It has horns."

At this point the pilot grows impatient and frustrated. He snatches back the notepad and makes a final drawing, this time of a box with three holes in it.

"Here is a box," says the pilot. "Your sheep is inside."

Finally, the boy is satisfied.

Most people with children, or those who have spent any time around children, or those who remember being children, will understand this story and find something familiar in it.

Like many parents, after spending a small fortune on an elaborate birthday gift for my child, I've been surprised to discover that he is far more interested in the cardboard packaging than the flashing, battery-powered toy within.

There's no real mystery to it. A box is the best kind of gift—a gift that can never disappoint. For the little prince, the hidden sheep in the box is far better than any singular, specific sheep that the pilot could draw. And while a flashing, battery-powered toy might be fun for certain purposes and for a limited amount of time, a box is good for any range of purposes and for an unlimited amount of time.

In the hands of a child, a cardboard box will be a home, a spaceship, a fort, a cave, a pirate ship, a castle, a robot, etc. What's more—the child doesn't have to choose. The fact that the box was one thing yesterday doesn't preclude it from being something else today.

Compare this to a toy car, which will only ever be a toy car.

A box achieves this amazing feat of versatility by being open. Its winning feature isn't the cardboard box but rather the empty space within. Empty space in which countless possibilities can take shape will *always* be more intriguing than a product with a single application. We could call this "The Cardboard Box Principal." When we embrace the fact that we're living *within* technology, we are playing with the box. When we see technology as something we live *with*, we are playing with the toy car. We will bump up against its limitations again and again.

Tech-as-Tool versus Tech-as-Space

When evaluating a new technology, one of the first meaningful questions one can ask is whether or not it operates as a tool or opens up a space. To understand the difference, think again of the box. Tech-as-tool is the shiny, plastic, battery-operated toy. Tech-as-space is the box.

With tech-as-tool one can always ask "What's it for?" or "What does it do?"

I experienced this firsthand when I co-founded WalkMe. WalkMe, operating as a space and not just a tool, can be hard to pitch. The elevator pitch would take a whole ride up and down the Chrysler Building to articulate because of the great range of what could happen in this technological space.

But while tech-as-tool may be more easily explained, it will always be limited. Tech-as-tool is a faulty model we have in our minds about how to interact with tech. In some cases this faulty model affects the products we use. Sometimes designers will create a product that truly is limited in its applications. In other cases, however, it's the mindset of the user and not the designer which causes the tech to be viewed as a tool. To illustrate my point, think back to the man using his smartphone as a calculator.

It's easy to get bogged down by this conception of tech because its alternative—tech-as-space—tends to be invisible. When we live within technology—are wholly immersed in it, and have fully adopted it—we lose the ability to see it.

Tech-as-tool is far more visible, and has influenced the way we think about invention and innovation. It has also affected the way we interact with our technology.

Here's how most of us think about innovation and invention: an inventor comes across a specific and narrow problem. The inventor then comes up with a brilliant technological patch for that problem. Perhaps he says, "I need to join these two pieces of wood together... but how?" Then, in a moment of inspiration, he has invented the nail. It is a perfect and singular solution to his perfect and singular problem.

But then... "How will I drive these nails into the wood?" He then invents a hammer. Another perfect tool for a singular application.

Plenty of individuals have made careers selling products that were invented this way: a carrot-shaped carrot peeler or a pancake-batter dispenser that gets you a perfectly shaped pancake every single time. These kinds of As-Seen-On-TV inventions are either cute, helpful, or ridiculous. Sometimes all three. They make great stocking-stuffers. But they tend not to endure the test of time.

The bottle opener opens bottles. The Swiss Army Knife however is a space in which countless possibilities can take shape—a bottle opener being one among these.

This is the difference between a phone and smartphone. A phone makes calls. But what does a smartphone do? The best answer to this question is the one that Apple put out for itself in one of its earliest iPhone ad campaigns. "There's an app for that." What does the iPhone do? Well—what do you want it to do? The smartphone is an open technological space, and much like the cardboard box is for children, and by far society's most beloved toy.

So far, I have talked about the difference between tech-as-tool and tech-as-space from a matter of design. There is an objective design difference between a cardboard box and a toy car, or between a bottle opener and a Swiss Army Knife.

When it comes to the enterprise technology that we use in large organizations, however, there are very few bottle openers out there. These are sophisticated technologies that continue to develop every day. They are spaces into which we can move, within which we can be immersed, and by which we can be transformed. What stops us, then, is not their design. It's our approach and our mindset coupled with the inherent challenges presented by the adoption process.

It's the issue of "use" that sums up our problem with adoption. Use takes skill. Use takes training. Use can become misuse or underuse. No one needs to "use" tech-as-space. We use a tool, we do not use a space—we operate within it.

I spoke about this issue with a Senior Account Executive at EMC. EMC, a leading worldwide provider of data storage solutions, made a shift from one CRM to Salesforce in 2009.

"It's a huge decision to make that kind of shift," recalled the exec. "When you're a sales-heavy company, with tens of thousands of individuals interfacing with customers and selling solutions all over the world, a change in CRM is a change in the way you do just about everything.

"Not to mention that these software solutions aren't just something you pick up at the store. There is a significant customization effort. Between shopping, customizing and implementing, the transition takes over a year and costs the company millions of dollars."

No business would opt for these difficulties if the tech wasn't well worth their time and effort. For EMC, the time for change had definitely come. It wasn't so much that they had outgrown their previous CRM, but rather that the old tech wasn't pushing them to grow.

"Every salesperson in the company had been doing things in their own individual way—with email, over the phone, with meetings, etc. They wouldn't be selling *through* the system. Instead, they would just sell how they sell and use the old CRM to log the information after the fact."

What EMC needed was a software that would do more for them than just log transactions. "You have this huge company with salespeople and operations all over the world and you wonder—how did we ever manage this without a good CRM?"

Obviously EMC was expecting huge business outcome out of the new CRM. Salesforce did more. It forecasts the year for individual salespeople and for the business as a whole. It coordinates between our projected sales and supply needs so that they can get our products where they need to be exactly when they need to be there.

The question is, do users use it as a tool to its maximum utilization? And do all Salespeople use it at the same level?

EMC has been operating within the new system for ten years now, but Schultz remembers the struggles of the adoption process and still sees these issues among certain users today.

"You always have people who are resistant. Either they're the old-school salespeople who don't like being told to do something in a new way, or they genuinely don't know how to use the technology. Maybe they only know how to use it the way we used to use the old CRM—logging their transactions but not getting as much out of it as they could."

"There's one tool which is part of the CRM that uses analytics to generate new sales opportunities. It will tell me which of my contacts is likely to be in the market to buy a certain product based on other purchases he or she has recently made. Maybe I could have made these sales without Salesforce—but it would have been a matter of luck. Perhaps I would have arrived at that contact in my Rolodex at the right time, but probably not. This tool, then, just put an opportunity for $400,000 into our pipeline.

"And then I talk to other employees and find out that they don't use this feature, or maybe that they don't even know that it's there. This happens a lot with new employees, and it's part of why we have a mentorship program."

But this Salesforce veteran will also admit that even he probably spends 80% of his time on 20% of the software's functionality.

"They have geniuses at work all the time making this tool, and they're making it *for me*—so that I can sell better. It's all there for me, but sometimes you see a button you don't recognize and you just move past it." Leadership needs to look to their new tech not only for its uses and applications, but also for its possibilities. When it comes to a CRM, leadership shouldn't ask "how can this speed up or organize what we are already doing?" but rather, "how can this technology transform our approach towards sales."

The Relationship

The first thing we need to do to improve our abilities with enterprise technology is to acknowledge that we are in a dynamic, ever-evolving relationship.

Take a moment to think about some of the different relationships in your life, whether they're romantic, familial, or platonic. When it comes down to it, no matter how special and individual each relationship in our life may be, there are some common issues that we face. Perhaps the biggest issue in relationships, is change.

All relationships are subject to change. They change because we change. While we may see ourselves as fixed, we're all changing and evolving all the time. While we're changing and evolving, so are the people around us and the world we live in.

So many relationships falter when one individual either can't or won't accept that the other person in the relationship has grown or changed in some way. What comes to mind for me is the relationship I have with my kids.

The relationship between parent and child is simultaneously incredibly fulfilling and hugely challenging. A big part of what makes it so challenging is that kids change so damn fast.

Taking care of an infant is hard, but it's not impossible. Eventually, you kind of start to figure it out. But at the exact moment you start patting yourself on the back and saying, "Hey, I've got this, in fact, I'm pretty good at it," your child has already changed into something else! It used to be that you could just lay the kid on a blanket with a few toys and he or she was all set—now they are moving around grabbing everything. The parental learning process begins again. There is incremental progress. And then suddenly, the kid has another birthday! Now your kid is two and you're back, in many ways, to square one. This cycle becomes more dramatic with time. By the time your kid is sixteen, you have sixteen years of experience raising this child, but zero experience raising a sixteen-year-old.

When I had my second kid, I remember thinking, "Well, this won't be so tough. After all, I still have my notes from round one somewhere around here." But while you may have more experience than you did the first time around, the challenge still feels new. This is, after all, a new child. It's also a new family, one in which there is already another kid. The dynamic has changed. You have changed. Your partner has changed. Maybe you've moved apartments. Maybe you have a new job. The circumstances are changing all around you and you start to panic.

"Will this ever be easy?"

That's the thing about relationships. If they were easy, we could go on autopilot. But they take continued awareness and evolution.

If it seems like a stretch to compare this kind of relationship to the relationship organizations have with their technology, think for a moment about the role technology plays in your life. It's not the same as a person, of course, but think of the disappointment and frustration you feel when your technology fails you. Think of the joys when it helps you solve a problem in a meaningful way. Think of the sheer amount of hours we spend interacting with technology. And think also of how the digital workplace has grown in the past decade from the infant it once was.

If this still does not register, consider Facebook. Every time Facebook makes a design change or adds a new feature, inevitably some petition circles around from user to user urging Facebook to go back to the way it was. No one likes change. It's funny, then, how after just a few short weeks no one can remember what Facebook looked like before the interface was updated.

Remember when all statuses had to start with "[Your Name] is…"?

It seems like a different lifetime.

When a technology makes a large design overhaul, the typical response of individuals is to moan about how it's terrible and to long for the good 'ole days of two weeks ago. This is not the attitude we want to see in our organizations. To embrace technology, we have to embrace change.

As much as we'd love for things to stay still (because then we could master what we're doing and go on autopilot), this is simply not the reality we live in. However, most of us are behaving as if it were.

Here's what people think happens when an organization makes the decision to adopt a new technology:

A problem or set of problems is identified. An appropriate technology is selected from amongst the available options to solve this problem. The technology is then purchased and customized. The staff is trained to use the new technology and then, voila, the problem or set of problems has been effectively solved.

We have to realize if we're going to get past the problems we have adopting tech, the above model, while it may be a lovely idea, is not what is actually happening.

Our current model of digital adoption has everything at rest, like fruit in a still life, when actually it's more like a fruit tree—blooming, ripening and rotting through the constant cycle of life.

To create a more accurate model of digital adoption we need to remember the principle of the "vicious cycle," and also remember that the movement experienced by large organizations – in which our problems, our tech, and our organizations themselves are in constant flux – is not something we can expect to change anytime soon.

The story of the banking industry can teach us a few things about this kind of movement. We had the opportunity to work with Bank of

Montreal as they navigated their own digital transformation and saw first-hand the multiple moving targets that the organization was chasing.

Traditionally, bank customers resolved issues through either a meeting, a trip to the bank, or a phone call. But as consumers become more and more dependent on digital interfacing, customers were no longer interested in waiting on the phone for help from a customer service representative. Bank of Montreal understood that it had to transform its consumer interface.

To solve this problem, Bank of Montreal began to reimagine how they handle customer-facing interactions using digital platforms. New technological solutions were implemented to address customer demands—but as we know, such technological patches can lead to additional challenges in the form of slow and awkward adoption.

What we see in Bank of Montreal's story is three kinds of change. There is the change of externally dictated needs when customers began to expect the convenience of digital options; there is change of the organization itself that occurred when the leadership chose to focus on digital transformation; and change of technology experienced when the tech that they had been using was no longer the best technology to serve their customers.

All three of these areas are liable to change—independent of each other, at different paces, and in different directions. It's a target moving in multiple dimensions.

Now that we've discussed the attitudes and perspectives necessary to skillfully navigate the adoption process—viewing technology as a space, embracing the principle of change—it's time to take a look at the strategies we will need to put these principles into action.

5 RETHINKING USER EXPERIENCE

The Digital Concierge and the UX Overlay

"Can you set an alarm for tomorrow at seven?"

"Your alarm is set."

"Thanks... and can you check what the weather will be like tomorrow in Chicago?"

"The weather will be 75 degrees and sunny."

"Ok, great. Thanks... goodnight!"

"You're very welcome."

Now of course I know that I don't have to say either "thanks" or "goodnight" to my phone. My politeness will not be appreciated by that machine any more than my rudeness would be taken with offense. But it just feels natural. After all, I've just had what resembles the most basic, human exchange of dialogue. A few questions asked and a few questions answered—as if I was at the concierge desk of a hotel requesting a wake-up call before my flight and inquiring genially about the weather.

At no point in the exchange did I feel like I was "using" my phone in the traditional sense. Perhaps I'm a bit spoiled. It's not like it's that hard to open the clock app and set an alarm for myself before opening up the weather app and glancing at the forecast for Chicago. But it doesn't matter how hard it is to open those apps. What matters is how easy it is to ask my question in the simple, natural way in which people ask questions of one another.

Voice recognition personal assistance programs like Google, Siri and Alexa are, in fact, remarkably similar to a hotel concierge. Not only can the concierge tell you what tours to take in a new city and what restaurants to go to, but he or she can also make the booking for you. The concierge can assist you with transportation, give you directions, and help you arrange your day. Each one of these tasks is probably something you can handle on your own, but each one would come with its own level of time commitment and you would find yourself hunched over your computer in the hotel room reading reviews on TripAdvisor in one tab, glancing at a map in another tab, and trying to figure out if you'd have enough time to do the riverboat architecture tour without missing your next reservation. Instead of having to sift through pages of information to figure out how to do these separate things, you simply voice your questions and receive answers or express what you'd like to do and have it arranged for you.

When you have this simple dialogue with the Google voice recognition program on your phone, all you have to do is express your needs. The effort of bouncing between apps gathering and synthesizing data from each one is done for you. These voice recognition programs are a luxury of the smartphone age. None of our phone apps—at least not on my phone—are very challenging to operate. Still, it's nice to have the luxury to stand aside and let the phone's concierge do the work.

For enterprise software, such a go-between would eliminate the most challenging of digital adoption issues. This kind of go-between would create a conceptual separation between the internal workings of the software platform and the experience of the user—just as the concierge stands between the traveler and the messiness of all those booking websites and maps.

As things stand right now—UX is an integral part of the platforms we use. And while the individual UX of any given platform continues to develop and become more intuitive, the burden remains on the user to skillfully learn how to navigate each individual software's platform.

The technology to separate the user experience from the underlying platform already exists and is driving a UX standardization across all platforms. I was fortunate to co-found WalkMe, which pioneered the Digital Adoption Platform market.

Digital Adoption Platforms (DAP) provide one interface across different software systems. They operate according to the logic of a navigation system. With a proactive navigation system, drivers don't need to remember directions, worry about getting lost, or waste time retracing their steps after missing an exit. They only need to know where they are going. Having input the address, the system will guide them there. Similarly, the Digital Adoption Platform is built to guide users to their "destinations," within a digital platform or across multiple platforms. All that the user will need to know is their end destination – or, similarly, what they are trying to achieve with the system at hand.

WalkMe's Digital Adoption Platform is built to adapt to the user rather than the user having to adapt to the system. In this way, the DAP provides contextual and proactive training based on previous insight into how the employee is using the system and where support is most needed for each user.

This market is expanding, due in large to the fact that leaders are now beginning to acknowledge the magnitude of the challenge of digital adoption and looking for ways to respond.

Maximizing Employee Potential and Productivity

Without a Digital Adoption Platform to encompass the workplace environment, we are asking our employees to become technicians of each and every software used within our organizations. Our teams then become unable to focus on their core work and instead find themselves spending time and energy becoming a software technician. With time and dedication, they may become very skilled. More often, however, this is not the case. They remain in a perpetual state of overwhelm and frustration. But even when we succeed in pushing employees to reach an IT-worthy level of technical savviness, we need to ask ourselves why we are doing this and what we are getting out of it. More important, we need to ask ourselves what we are losing in the process.

I spoke to a young man in New York named Albert about his experience painstakingly learning the ins and outs of his organization's software. His story is a lot like that of Denise. He may not call himself an old model or be afraid of technology, but he's not a Super User either. He has a casual relationship with technology and a casual level of competency. In short, this is not his passion.

Instead, Albert is passionate about the environment. Throughout high school and university he worked on and off at organic farms. He studied environmental policy and founded campus initiatives to make his campus greener. In the process, he learned a great deal both about policy and about leadership—priming him for a number of great employment opportunities after he graduated with a Master's Degree in environmental policy.

Post-graduation, Albert moved away from the leafy green of the campus to a new kind of ecosystem—New York City. There he was snatched up quickly by a prominent non-profit organization working in environmental policy and advocacy.

Here's where Albert's story becomes very similar to that of Denise, our "old model." Technology was not a topic in any of Albert's interviews with the organization's leadership, and yet, as soon as he was onboarded, becoming a software specialist of the organization's internal platforms became priority number one.

Management seemed blissfully unaware that digital adoption could ever be an issue. Training was scant for a new employee, yet it was expressed to Albert on numerous occasions that his usage of the internal software systems needed to be flawless.

Albert happens to be the type who proves himself quickly in sink or swim situations like these. Through a mix of methods including asking his coworkers for help, watching online tutorials, and exploring the systems thoroughly, he eventually got the hang of it. He had successfully passed the first crucible of post-graduate employment—one that very few individuals in the job market can avoid—he joined the army of technicians.

Here lies a troubling disconnect. For many employees, such technical knowledge is simply not connected to their core work, expertise or passion. Albert's passion was born outdoors and nourished by summers of working with his hands in the soil. His knowledge extends from the nooks and crannies of complex international environmental policies to the inner workings of bee hives and ant hills. Albert, for all these reasons, is unique. So why is this environmental policy expert being used as a software technician? Is this really the best use of his unique expertise and experience?

It's not just Albert, though. Every single employee is unique. They've been chosen for their current position by a combination of passion, life experience, education and work experience particular to them alone. And yet all these employees are being asked to join the same assembly line—becoming technicians of software systems that often distract them or hinder them from putting their talents to use.

When we're dealing with this on a large scale, for example with an enterprise employing thousands and adopting multiple software systems, we have a productivity issue. A study we conducted at WalkMe discovered that most employees spend at least 1.5 hours per week dealing with errors they have made as a result of using a specific platform to perform a single process, coming out to 77 hours each year. Apply this math to an organization with thousands of employees and we're talking about a cost of millions, for one system and one process only.

The more software systems in use, of course, combined with a larger number of staffers, results in a correspondingly large productivity loss. Our salespeople will be interacting with their CRM at times when they should be interacting with their clients, and our HR departments will find themselves inputting data when they could be dealing with actual humans.

But the issue can run even deeper than productivity—affecting a company's morale in a way that flows outward towards consumers. This idea was put forth by Verizon's CIO, Vic Bhagat, who explained on a recent podcast called "The Modern Customer" exactly how a frustrating computer system at a call center will lead to a frustrated call center representative, who is fielding the calls of (very often) already frustrated consumers.

Office Suite

I'd like to broaden my metaphor of the hotel concierge from before. In fact, it's not only the concierge that operates as a go-between between the internal workings of what we're trying to do and the guest's experience—actually, the entire hotel operates on this principal.

This is why staying in a hotel is one of the most pampering experiences that human beings have devised for ourselves. Ok, yes, today there are alternatives such as Airbnb, but they have not entirely eliminated the unique experience of staying in a hotel.

After a day of sightseeing, you can return to your room and find it restored to factory settings. This process goes unseen for the hotel guest. All the guest knows is that the bed is made, the little cups in the bathroom have been turned over once again, and the toilet paper has been folded into a small triangle. How nice! If you want a late-night snack at a hotel, all you need to do is call room service. No need to swipe your card or pull out your wallet (except to give a tip) as the meal will be automatically charged to the room.

People pay big for this kind of service and it's easy to understand why. Travelling can be strenuous. Many hotel guests are travelling for business purposes, and if their days aren't loaded up with meetings, they are tourists exhausting themselves on their vacations by walking around the city all day. It makes perfect sense that these travelers want to solely focus on what they've come to this city to get done. Business or pleasure, this is the core purpose of their travel. Why bother fussing with all the small details?

For this exact reason, we need to feel that our technology at work is taking care of us the way we would be taken care of in a nice hotel. We are not at work for the purposes of learning how to use a dozen different online platforms. The reasons we are at work are too numerous to count.

They are deeply unique—connected to both the individual organization and each individual employee.

6 TUNING INTO TECH

The Ideal Loop

A UX overlay, with its ability to smooth UX across platforms and revolutionize the way we train and offer support, is only one aspect of what our digital adoption technology can provide for us. Equally important, however, is the foundation of a functional feedback loop.

But what kind of feedback do we need? Let's look at the four main qualities of a functioning feedback loop so that we can begin to understand how such a system would be put in place for digital adoption.

Ongoing Feedback

Ideal feedback is ongoing. Feedback provides meaningful data continuously or at very regular intervals. This is important because a feedback loop needs to create opportunities for leadership to intervene with meaningful action.

For most of us, this is obvious. We put this principle to practice all the time in our organizations. Think of how an organization manages its finances. Through regular monitoring, businesses keep close tabs on their financial wellbeing. Is the company making money, losing money, or breaking even? Are there cash flow issues? This information is necessary for making day-to-day decisions as well as big picture plans.

When a new technology is first rolled out, no one on the staff has any habits yet for using it. This means no good habits or bad habits. This is an incredibly valuable time! If we don't get any feedback until six months or a year after the technology is introduced, we have lost out on this window of opportunity. Bad habits will have been formed, and we all know how hard those can be to break.

Non-Binary Feedback

An ideal feedback loop is non-binary. This means that it's providing us with quality data that goes beyond any binary evaluation of "good," or "bad."

A binary feedback loop can be understood like a pass/fail grading system at a high school. Students finish the semester with a "P" or an "F." But what do these letters tell us?

They do not tell us whether the student has enjoyed the class, whether the student barely understands the material at all, or whether the student is extremely strong in some areas while being weak in others. If the student failed, it doesn't tell us why or in what way.

Likewise, when we attempt to adopt tech, what do we want to learn about the relationship our staff is having with that tech? When we get feedback about this relationship, what does it really tell us if this information is binary and all we know about each employee is that they either "use the tech" or "don't use the tech?"

If we establish that an employee is using the tech, we still won't know if they find it useful, if it has helped create opportunities for them, if they are using it for a broad or a narrow range of applications, or if they are using it only to appease the management without seeing its purpose within a broader context.

Meaningful feedback, then, should be non-binary. It shouldn't merely tell us "yes" or "no," but rather "how, why, how much, when, and what."

Seamless Feedback

What's the best exercise a person can do to stay in optimal shape?

Some people will answer this by saying running. Some will say swimming. Some will say yoga. Some will say skydiving.

The truth is much simpler than this. The best workout is the one you actually do. After all, if you just don't have the time or the money for a pool membership, what good will it do you to know that swimming is the best workout. It's not the best workout for you.

A workout regime, for individuals who are slightly resistant to exercising, needs to be easy. Not easy to do, but easy to access. If you have to travel too far to the gym, you may never get there. But if you discover that it's easy for you to just slip on your jogging shoes and head out the door, that's one less obstacle.

The point is that we should try to reduce obstacles that add more effort to this already effort-heavy practice. The same is true of a healthy feedback system.

If possible, receiving feedback should be seamless. If it involves a lot of manual check-ins, tooth pulling from employees, and time, leadership will be less motivated to do it regularly. A feedback system should happen automatically rather than manually. Feedback should be woven into the fabric of operations in such a way that it can happen without obstacles and exhaustion.

While we already have many systems in place providing analytics and feedback about customer experience and behavior, most large organizations are sorely lacking feedback that is employee-focused: providing metrics and data on employee behavior with vital internal technology.

It is just as important to apply these analytical principles to employees as it is for us to analyze customer behavior. For employees trying their best to do their work within the systems and platforms required of them, such data could help leadership fulfill its role, which is to support employees as they fulfill their roles – doing their core work without unnecessary stress and obstacles.

But creating a feedback loop which is ongoing, non-binary and seamless is just the beginning of the journey towards successful digital adoption. It will create the framework for organizational awareness: awareness of where your employees are stuck, what processes they find difficult to complete, when they need help, or why they are not productive. This is the insight we need to gain while using digital systems.

Actionable Feedback

Imagine that your car's gas gauge only told you that you were running low at the last possible minute, without enough fuel to make it to the nearest station. The fact that the light goes on and flashes means you have feedback. You know the data is correct, and you know what you need to do about it, but you are not able to act on that knowledge. This kind of feedback is not actionable.

Actionable feedback is a set of suggestions that are relevant, timely, and available at regular intervals. Without leading to a course of action, it doesn't matter if feedback is seamless, non-binary, and ongoing - we won't be able to turn this data into anything of use. Our ability to respond is the most crucial part of the feedback loop.

7 UNLOCKING POTENTIAL

Beginning the process of new software adoption is never a decision made lightly. Because of the significant cost and time investment, leadership at large organizations will only roll out a new system if they truly believe it has the potential to revolutionize business processes and help the organization grow towards its goals.

At most large organizations we are dealing with a significant number of such systems, and while the sheer volume of them may be overwhelming to employees who have to be trained on each one, we can assume each system is, in its own way, vital to the organization's trajectory. As we add more and more of these systems to our organizations, the work of our employees becomes more complex. But, this complexity offsets the benefits of these new systems.

Here is where the digital concierge becomes so vital. Just as your smartphone's voice recognition personal assistance program belongs to no app in particular, this second layer over our software platforms is shared by all of them. A DAP is the universal standard of user experience between platforms, allowing organizations to make use of the wide range of software systems available to us without operations becoming needlessly complex as a result.

With a Digital Adoption Platform in place, all that the employees would need to know is what they want to do within the platform. They would not be expected to be technicians of the platform. The only expertise required of them would be the expertise for which they were hired—that which is connected to their core work. Unlike Denise and

Albert who discovered that technology became their main concern when starting at their new jobs, employees working with the support of a DAP would be able to live within their tech, and thus forget about it!

This is the value of living within technology:

To be within something, to a certain extent, allows you to forget it exists.

Leadership, however, cannot and should not forget technology. We need to make it a priority. It is one of the most important areas of focus for us, and in many ways we have been failing to treat it as such. But when it comes to our employees—all those individuals who are using the many software systems required by their work on a daily basis—forgetting is exactly what we want to happen.

Again, think of the hotel. Management at large organizations is like management of the hotel. They need to stay aware of the internal operations—the cleaning crew, the kitchen, the concierge, the utilities, etc. But the guests (our employees) should be comfortably taken care of and able to focus on other things—namely the work they were hired to do.

Right now our employees are unable to forget technology. Our hotel is operating more like a guest house where you have to do daily chores to earn your keep. This is where we lose out on human potential. Users should be occupied with their core work, not with their tools. Their tools, meanwhile, should be operating as silent, facilitative partners.

We stand to earn twice: once on the potential of the tech and again on the human potential of those individuals using it.

When the Shoe Fits

"When the shoe fits, the foot is forgotten," said the Chinese philosopher Chang Tzu.

In the same spirit, a technology adopted when everyone has forgotten about it —when its use is so natural that it can go unnoticed, like the chairs we sit on and the clocks on the wall.

When the shoe fits, we are at last free to make use of it. To *go somewhere*.

The same is true of technology. But we can never know where tech can take us until it is adopted.

Inventors, even the greatest among them, rarely know what they are truly inventing. This is because an invention is a stand-alone thing: the product of one mind or a team of minds. In this sense, it is limited in its potential. An invention's true potential never even reveals itself until it is adopted.

The automobile, for example, was a revolutionary invention. But as a stand-alone invention, it's not much more than a horseless carriage.

But as cars were adopted, we adapted. We built highways, we changed our approach to urban planning and development, and we reconfigured how we sell and shop (no one is going to a big box store if they can't load up their trunk afterwards). Our culture morphed. Jack Kerouac wrote his paean to the American highway, "On the Road," and getting one's driver's license became the ultimate symbol of coming-of-age and independence.

Surely Karl Benz knew his invention was important – but I don't think it's ever possible to predict what the true potential will look like or feel like until the tech is adopted.

Unlocking this potential is our true goal. The end game of software adoption has never just been only the technology itself. The idea is to unlock potential that we can't yet imagine. We'll only be able to imagine it when it surrounds us – when we are operating so thoroughly within our technology that we can forget it and move on to bigger and far greater things.

ABOUT REPHAEL SWEARY

Rephael Sweary, cofounded WalkMe, the leading digital adoption platform, in 2011. Previously, Rafi was the Co-founder, CEO, and then President of Jetro Platforms which was acquired in 2007. Since then, he has funded and helped build a number of companies both in his role as Entrepreneur-in-Residence at Ocean Assets and in a personal capacity.

www.ingramcontent.com/pod-product-compliance
Lightning Source LLC
Chambersburg PA
CBHW040325220526
45473CB00009B/2579